Contents

WHAT'S IN THIS KIT

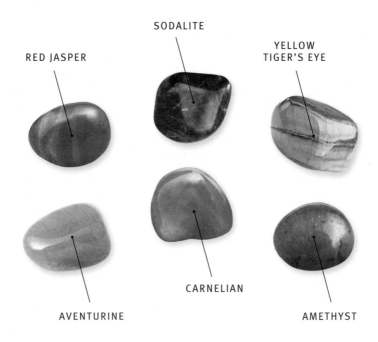

SODALITE

RED JASPER

YELLOW TIGER'S EYE

AVENTURINE

CARNELIAN

AMETHYST

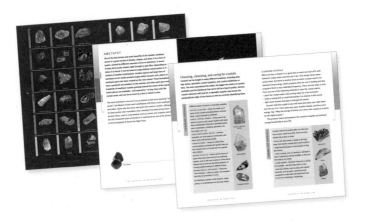

64-PAGE ILLUSTRATED GUIDEBOOK

INTRODUCTION

Colorful as the rainbow and sparkling with light, crystals, precious stones, and minerals have fascinated people since the beginning of time. Unusual and precious stones were picked up or dug out of the earth by our ancestors to be worn as ornaments or carried as amulets for protection. Throughout history, beautiful stones have been exchanged, fought over, collected, used as healing tools, or worn as exquisite jewelry, and today interest in crystals and minerals is still as popular as ever.

Why are crystals so fascinating? Perhaps because of their sheer diversity—they come in so many colors, shapes, and sizes; perhaps because they all come from the earth itself, miraculously formed inside its crust, and they remind us of the mystery and beauty of our planet. Perhaps because they are rare and beautiful and seem to reach out to us with their presence. When people come into contact with crystals they want to touch them, hold them, and feel their shape, sensing their texture. Examples such as deep purple amethyst, rich yellow tiger's eye, sparkling green aventurine, or swirling blue sodalite all have unique appeal. Very often the colors of the stones themselves are the main attraction.

This book explores the world of crystals by linking to their variations in color. In order to understand stones from this perspective, the different bands of color in the spectrum will be shown individually, and their importance in color healing will be explained. Light, when split into the different bands of color, is a very important source of information to the eye and the brain, and in the twenty-first century, color healing is coming into its own as a source of regeneration for body, mind, and spirit. Linking crystals to color is a wonderful way to begin exploring how they can rebalance and restore energy. In this book, you will find detailed information on the six crystals in this kit, so you can read about their geology and their uses, how to care for them and place them in your environment.

As soon as you hold a crystal in your hand you connect with the earth, opening the way to new discoveries. Enjoy your journey.

The World of Color

Color has a profound effect on how we react to our surroundings. If we wake up to gray skies and rain for several days, it can be depressing. Then if suddenly there is a bright blue sky outside, the leaves on the trees look very green, the sunlight brings out the colors of flowers, and our moods begin to change as a result. All this is due to the way we perceive color through the eyes, our organs of sight. The eye is a sophisticated light box that allows us to receive and interpret different shades of color. Light frequencies also have very real effects on the brain, influencing our internal chemistry. The gift of sight and the ability to enjoy colors is crucial to the way we perceive and react to the world around us. In this chapter, we will explore in detail how the eye reacts to color, breaking down the seven colors of the rainbow into more varied shades, and find out how color healing uses different shades for specific effects on body and mind. This will help us connect later in the book with all the variations in colors present in crystals and minerals.

What is color and how do we see it?

The eyes allow color to be perceived and interpreted by the brain. They account for approximately 70 percent of our total sensory perception, not only of color but also perspective and distance. Their ability to filter and interpret light contributes to the majority of our everyday experiences, because what we see influences how we feel and react in almost every moment.

LIGHT AND THE EYES

The main rays of the color spectrum appear in a rainbow—red, orange, yellow, green, blue, indigo, and violet—when sunlight splits white light into colors by shining through rain droplets. There are other bands of light our eyes cannot see, such as ultraviolet rays from sunlight and infrared rays used in security systems or in the remote control of your television. Electric light is artificially created, and operates mainly in the visible part of the spectrum.

Over millions of years of evolution, our eyes and brains have become used to interpreting color. Reds, oranges, and yellows appear warm to us, and they have a stimulating or energizing effect; greens, blues, and violets are cooler hues, with a more soothing effect. Although we live in artificial environments, we still long for outdoor landscapes filled with blue sky, and we enjoy the colors of flowers balanced by green leaves. For thousands of years before the invention of electric light, the rhythms of our lives were far more governed by the presence or absence of natural light, and the effects of light on our eyes dictated how we lived.

An expanded color wheel

Traditional representations of the color wheel show seven shades found in the rainbow—red, orange, yellow, green, blue, indigo, and violet. However, close examination of an actual rainbow in the sky shows that the main bands of color are not distinct; they merge into each other. So, for example, from deep green the color slowly changes to turquoise—blue and green mixed together—to aquamarine, to pale blue, and then into the pure blue shades. This gradual bleed of color creates a whole new palette of more subtle shades, all of which are represented in the range of available crystals.

THE EXPANDED SPECTRUM

Twenty shades are represented here, including tones such as brown, which is linked very much to the physical earth, and silver-gray, exemplified by the metal silver, yellow-gold to include the metallic element gold, and even black, the opposite to white in the spectrum. Black is a very important resonant shade in healing, and does not always have negative associations, being seen rather as a cleansing vibration. White is the shade that encompasses all the colors of the spectrum.

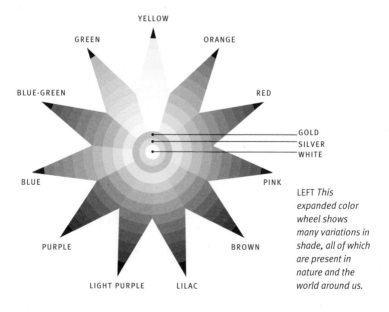

LEFT *This expanded color wheel shows many variations in shade, all of which are present in nature and the world around us.*

Color healing

Every day, thanks to our sun, living on the earth means that we are literally bathed in full-spectrum light, that is, the colors we can see plus invisible rays, such as ultraviolet and infrared. Scientific research has shown that we need to be exposed to full daylight for at least twenty minutes each day to maintain an ideal internal balance of the body's chemistry. Inside the brain are special centers that respond to light—including the pineal and pituitary glands that control the body's hormonal balance.

Lack of exposure to full daylight can have detrimental effects on health. Modern life is lived mostly indoors, away from full natural sunlight, trapped under artificial electric lighting. Medical conditions—including depression, poor sleep, low energy, and mood swings—can be caused by lack of sunlight, and this is sometimes called Seasonal Affective Disorder (SAD). Exposure to full-spectrum light for several hours daily is enough to correct many of these symptoms.

BELOW *The visible rainbow contains the seven major colors of the spectrum as well as many other delicate shades that blend into each other.*

THE EFFECTS OF COLORED LIGHT

Color healing directs light in different spectrum colors directly onto or into the body. Application of specific colors, either directly with equipment or visualized by the therapist, can bring about speedy and effective rebalancing of the body's energies. Red light has both a warming and stimulating effect and can raise blood pressure. Orange shades are energizing; yellow, which simulates the rise of the sun in the sky, awakens mental awareness. Green light has a soothing effect, calming the breathing. Relaxation responses increase in the presence of blue shades of light, and as these shades darken they simulate night falling and bring on a sense of sleepiness. All colors of the spectrum have their own vibrational frequency, and when they are directed at the body they are absorbed, leading to a wide variety of effects.

Some practitioners use color lamps or machines to project light through crystals to shine rays of true color onto the body. These have been scientifically shown to ease many physical problems. Emerald green light, for example, can help to heal broken bones and regenerate tissue, and ruby red light can raise body temperature and increase the metabolic rate. Blue light can have a healing effect on burns or damaged skin, while psychological or mental issues benefit from antidepressant orange and apricot shades, and pink lowers aggression.

AMETHYST

RED JASPER

YELLOW
TIGER'S EYE

AVENTURINE

SODALITE

10

Crystals and color

We have seen that light, split into the colors of the spectrum, can have noticeable effects on body and mind. Light is energy. Light projected through crystalline structures can be even more powerful, as used in some lasers, in which rubies or sapphires are used to create highly concentrated beams of light particles. Crystals reflect different colors because of their mineral composition; they attract us because of that color, their shape, and their beauty. In this way, it can be said that the mineral kingdom communicates with us.

HOW CRYSTAL COLOR IS USED

Over thousands of years of handling, wearing, and use, different crystals and minerals have become associated with particular healing effects. One example is bloodstone, a dark green agate flecked with red. The dramatic appearance of those red specks reminded people of blood, so the stone was carried by warriors because it was said to stop blood flowing from wounds. This could be regarded as mere superstition, but sometimes a powerful belief can bring about real results.

These days people's experiences of crystals are very individual. For example, a businesswoman working in a stressful, high-powered job never thought for a moment that something like a crystal could help her to relax. A friend gave her a piece of rose quartz; instinctively she responded to its color and started sleeping with it under her pillow. Suddenly her rest improved dramatically. Rose quartz is known to have extremely gentle healing effects on the whole system.

BLOODSTONE

In the same way that different rays of color have different effects, if you are particularly drawn to, for example, green stones, it is likely that you need green energy in your life, perhaps some healing around your emotions. Choosing crystals based on color is a simple way to begin exploring the mineral kingdom and find out more about yourself and your energy needs.

ROSE QUARTZ

The World of Crystals

This chapter explores the mineral kingdom of Earth, showing how the planet we live on is in a constant state of change, and how the dynamic and powerful creative cycles of the earth cause crystals to grow inside it. We will also look at different crystalline structures, as well as different groups of crystals, to find out about the processes that created them. This brings in elements of geology, the study of how the earth was formed, and mineralogy, the study of the elements that make up crystals and precious metals.

It is important to recognize the precious nature of these rare minerals and treat them with respect. It is easy to forget that the reason they can be obtained is because they have been taken out of the earth, sometimes by direct human intervention. Staying aware of the processes that created crystals in the first place helps you develop a respect for the crystals you decide to collect. Whether you simply have them in your space, wear them, or use them for healing purposes, they are still the gifts of the earth.

The dynamic forces of the earth

Earth is a planet subjected to dynamic forces that constantly change its structure, thanks to the intense heat at its molten core. This heat causes chemical reactions between minerals; these are natural, inorganic chemical substances and approximately 2,500 different types exist. The mineral kingdom provides the chemical building blocks for everything on the earth: rocks, plants, animals—and human beings.

THE THREE MAIN TYPES OF ROCK

IGNEOUS • Igneous rocks can be formed either underground or above ground. Underground, when melted rock deep within the earth, called magma, becomes trapped in small pockets, it cools to become rock. Igneous rocks also form when volcanoes erupt, pushing molten lava up through fissures and cracks to the earth's surface; as this cools, crystals and rocks are formed.

When combined with water just below the surface, magma may form quartz crystals in large gaps called veins; depending on the minerals present, other gems, such as aquamarine, may also appear.

METAMORPHIC • These are rock layers that have been changed after their original formation, usually by increases in pressure, heat, water vapor, or chemical reactions. Layers of clay and sand sinking into the crust under pressure can form the mineral compound corundum, appearing as sapphire or ruby.

SEDIMENTARY • Sedimentary rocks are formed when deposits of material—plant, animal, or inanimate—are subjected to pressure, so squeezing out all the fluids and turning them into solid layers. The most common sedimentary rock is sandstone.

The structure of crystals

Most crystals are made up of highly structured and ordered patterns of molecules called lattices. They take on a stable and regular pattern repeated again and again through their internal structure, creating shapes and facets with particular types of symmetry. Some of them form within layers of rock, others inside large bubbles of gas so the crystals grow from the outside toward the center of the space. Factors such as pressure, temperature, and rate of cooling influence the shape a crystal will eventually take. The classification of typical crystal shapes is shown in the table below.

CRYSTAL LATTICES

CUBIC • made up of three equal axes forming a cube—examples are pyrite, diamond, and fluorite

PYRITE

HEXAGONAL • four axes creating a six-fold symmetry—examples are emerald and aquamarine

TETRAGONAL • resembling two four-sided pyramids joined at the base—examples are apophyllite and zircon

ORTHORHOMBIC • three axes at 90 degrees to each other—examples are peridot and topaz

MONOCLINIC • three unequal axes creating an elongated shape—examples are gypsum or kunzite

TRICLINIC • the most asymmetric shape— examples are labradorite or turquoise

LABRADORITE

TRIGONAL • an elongated lozenge shape—examples are sapphire, tourmaline, and calcite

HARDNESS OF MINERALS

In 1812 a German mineralogist called Friedrich Mohs created a scale to help identify relative hardness in minerals. Hardness is a particular factor in jewelry making; only the hardest stones, such as corundum—ruby or sapphire—topaz, or diamond, are able to be faceted, that is, cut into shapes that allow them to reflect even more light so they sparkle. Softer stones shatter, which is why they tend to be simply smoothed and polished for setting in jewelry.

MOHS SCALE				
	HARDNESS	MINERAL	HARDNESS	MINERAL
	1	talc (softest)	6	moonstone
	2	gypsum	7	quartz
	3	calcite	8	topaz
	4	fluorite	9	ruby
	5	apatite	10	diamond (hardest)

OTHER FACTORS

Another classification, amorphous, is applied to specimens of organic origin such as amber, a fossilized tree resin, which does not have an internal geometric structure. Another type of amorphous stone is volcanic glass, called obsidian, which is formed when lava cools rapidly. Crystals are also assessed for their color, their luster—an inner quality, making them look

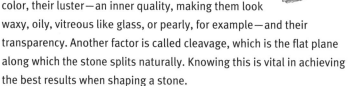

SNOWFLAKE OBSIDIAN

waxy, oily, vitreous like glass, or pearly, for example—and their transparency. Another factor is called cleavage, which is the flat plane along which the stone splits naturally. Knowing this is vital in achieving the best results when shaping a stone.

Because crystals take form in an astonishing variety of shapes and sizes, it is rare to find perfect examples of the geometric shapes on page 22, but the more you examine the stones you buy, the more you will recognize some of these characteristics.

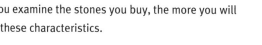

Main crystal groups

In mineralogy, the many types of crystals are classified into groups according to their chemical composition. The main groups shown on this page cover the kinds of crystals and minerals most commonly collected by crystal enthusiasts.

OXIDES • aluminum oxide forms the compound corundum, the red and blue forms of which are rubies and sapphires respectively; chrysoberyl, available mainly in golden yellow, is a beryllium aluminum oxide

NATIVE ELEMENTS • (pure metals): gold, silver, platinum, copper, carbon (as diamond), and titanium

SULFIDES • (metal plus sulfur): iron and sulfur forms pyrite, also called fool's gold

SILICATES • the main category is silicon dioxide, which makes quartz: clear quartzes—amethyst, rose quartz, smoky quartz, citrine, tourmalinated quartz, rutilated quartz; in microcrystalline quartzes, masses of tiny crystals appear in carnelian, agates, moss agate, and chalcedony, and these have a more waxy luster than clear quartz

also within this group are feldspars, comprising a huge number of crystals that are very common, including moonstone and labradorite

other large silicate groups are garnets, which may be rich in aluminum, iron, or chromium, depending on their location, and tourmaline and the beryls, including aquamarine or emerald, as well as the spodumenes, including kunzite

MINERALOIDS • tektites, such as moldavite, with a glasslike amorphous structure

ORGANIC MINERALS • organic, when talking about crystals, means a mineral that has plant or animal origins—amber, for example, is the fossilized resin of an ancient pine tree; pearls form when a grain of sand irritates the inner lining of the pearl oyster; and jet is a form of highly compressed coal

16

The Crystal Color Directory

This chapter contains individual entries covering the crystals in this kit. In each entry, you will find geological data about the stone, its composition, and its most common sources, as well as its hardness and other physical characteristics. Traditional associations and uses of the crystals in healing is also covered. The crystals are grouped according to the shades of color in which they most often occur; any variations are also noted.

As well as color associations, you will also find links to history and/or crystal healing applications. This information is given so that you can explore and learn about the stones from different perspectives. Consider, interpret, and feel your way into the descriptions; learn to trust your intuition. Remember that human beings and crystals are made up of different types of energy, but we live on the same planet and we just take different forms. If a particular type of stone attracts your attention, then it represents something you need to rebalance your system.

THE RED RAY

Red is a deeply vibrant and powerful vibration. In color healing, it is used to improve the circulation and raise blood pressure. Red is challenging, strong, physical; it is the color of blood, the liquid that symbolizes our life force, the transporter of oxygen and minerals, nutrients, and hormones to every cell of the body. Red brings us into the arena of physical life, the physical body, and the business of survival. "Nature, red in tooth and claw" is a phrase that sums up this powerful energy.

Sometimes, in the pursuit of spiritual enlightenment, the basic, rooted, and powerful energy of red is pushed aside in favor of more "heady" and ethereal color vibrations. Red is seen as too primitive, too linked to our basic instincts. Yet these instincts keep us alive, and they are a powerful source of inner connection in themselves. Red is the blood of birth and the monthly blood of females, whose cycles are governed by the phases of the moon—the blood of creation. Creative processes can be very powerful, sometimes even painful, but they bring about a sense of incredible achievement.

The seven chakras

In healing, red is associated with an energy center called the root chakra. There are seven major chakra centers in the body, situated at the coccyx/ tailbone, the sacrum, the solar plexus area under the rib cage, in the center of the chest, the throat, the center of the forehead, and at the crown of the head. Each of these centers has a color, usually seen as following the rainbow sequence of colors. Red is the color that energizes the root chakra and enhances the physical life force in the body.

Red crystals, such as garnet or ruby, have a powerful effect on the physical body, often bringing a sense of warmth, stimulation, and comfort. In healing, they are used to generate more energy in the system if life force is low. Physical, mental, or environmental stresses can cause damage to the body, the precious vehicle we rely on to keep us alive, so making us feel cold, depleted, and lacking in energy when everyday demands take over. The rich luster and vibration of red stones renew our strength and our ability to take our lives into our own hands, make decisions, and take action.

RED JASPER

Jaspers are a varied group of stones. They occur in many different colors due to different balances of minerals combined with microcrystalline quartz. They are often slightly dappled in appearance because of the tiny quartz crystals inside their structure, with an astonishing variation of specks and stripes, depending on the particular combinations of minerals mixed with their basic structure of silicon dioxide.

Red jasper is colored by hematite (iron oxide) and it is found in massive natural formations. The color is really emphasized when it is polished. As far back as Roman times, jasper was used in exterior mosaics as well as stone cladding for the insides of buildings; it was also combined with marble to create magnificent floors. In St. Petersburg, Russia, there are a number of churches with entire columns carved from jasper in different shades, including red, black, and gray. It is a relatively hard stone, being a member of the quartz family, so it can be carved into any number of shapes. It is a favorite for creating personal seals and seal rings carrying a crest or motif.

Healing uses of red jasper concentrate on the raising of energies, increasing the ability to cope with all of life's pressures. It is seen as a strengthening and life-enhancing stone. It also enhances the root chakra, creating a connection with the earth. It is very soothing used in the bath along with other gentle stones, such as green aventurine, to support the system if energy is low.

RAW

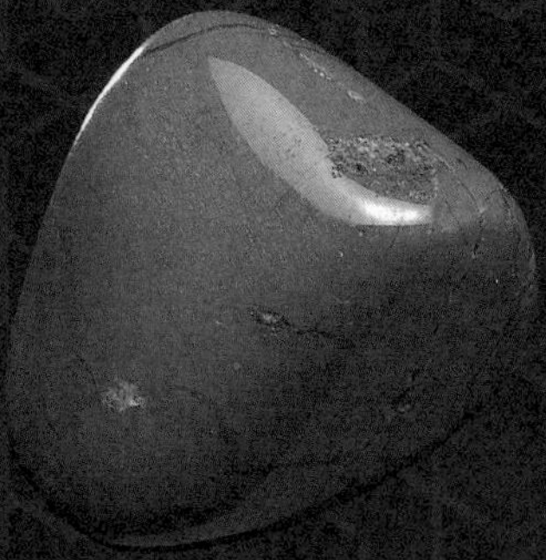

RED JASPER

FORM AND STRUCTURE
microcrystalline quartz in a
trigonal structure

opaque appearance with a
dense color

COLOR
red, also yellow, brown

GEOGRAPHICAL SOURCES
Brazil, France, Germany, Russia,
USA

RARITY
easily obtained and inexpensive
in large pieces, carved globes, or
small tumblestones

HARDNESS
6.5

PHYSICAL/EMOTIONAL USES
is gently energizing and
supportive, grounding and
protecting the body and
strengthening the energy field

energizes the circulation and
warms the system

promotes self-belief and the
courage to act

HEALING EFFECTS
in healing layouts, it can be
used on the root chakra or laid
in a circle around the body to
strengthen the energy field,
especially after a period of illness

PERSONAL USES
place under the pillow to
facilitate lucid dreaming

hold a tumblestone in each hand
to stabilize and balance energy

THE ORANGE RAY

From soft apricot shades to the vibrant color of the ripe fruit carrying its name, orange is one of the most cheering of all colors. It immediately conjures up images of summer vacations, spending time outdoors, or perhaps the taste and smell of the fruit on the tongue. Advertisements for orange juice frequently show happy people in the sunshine because the color and the fruit are associated with light and freedom. Children enjoy the color and taste of orange, and many adults need more orange energy to encourage a childlike sense of playfulness and spontaneity.

Orange is associated with the sacral chakra, which sits at the triangular sacrum bone at the base of the spine. This chakra energy is warming, stimulating, and antidepressant; it is also said to tone the reproductive organs. Orange energy is a combination of red (root chakra, connection with the earth, physical power) and yellow (solar plexus chakra, mental expansion and concentration). It builds confidence and the power of true expression within relationships, whether with the self or with others. Orange is needed when life seems dreary, when you need a pick-me-up, when you are stuck in fear, or feeling the effects of the middle of winter. Bright orange shades can be too stimulating, but softer, more muted apricot- or peach-colored shades are alternatives. They energize the sacral chakra energy more gently. Intuitive color healers will mute the orange ray according to their patient's needs.

The color of the sun

In some parts of the world orange and orange-gold colors have a special significance. In some Asian countries—India, Sri Lanka, and Thailand, for example—monks wear robes dyed in these shades because they are the color of falling leaves and, therefore, a symbol of letting go and nonattachment. Wreaths of orange or gold flowers are draped over statues of the gods; these are associated with the sun in all its changing moods, from the glow of sunrise or sunset to the brighter light of midday. In northern-European herbal medicine, the orange-colored flower called marigold, or calendula, was a favorite with early herbalists, such as the Englishman John Gerard. In the sixteenth century, he associated it with the sun and an ability to strengthen the spirits.

Orange crystals are a popular choice for jewelry because they are cheering and warming shades, enlivening any colors. In healing, these colored stones are used to help heal emotional imbalance and enhance self-confidence in emotional expression.

CARNELIAN

Carnelian is one of the most commonly available microcrystalline quartzes. Known as agate or chalcedony, it is made up of silicon dioxide colored by different levels of iron impurities, with specks, banding, or stripes in many shades of brown or orange-red. The stone itself has a beautiful warm orange color that is best appreciated when it is polished. It is available in a variety of shapes and sizes, as natural tumblestones or larger carved spheres or eggs.

Since ancient times, carnelian has been polished and worn as jewelry. The Egyptians used it to contrast with onyx and lapis lazuli in the making of collars and necklaces. The Romans were fond of it set in gold, using small beads in earrings or larger polished stones in finger rings for men and women. Because carnelian is a hard stone, it can be carved; examples of Roman signet rings or cameo rings survive from the early second century CE with exquisitely fashioned personal emblems or figures of gods. In the Middle Ages, carnelian was also popular as a healing stone. It was said to dissolve anger or rage, protect the wearer from negative influences, and promote courage.

Many people choose carnelian in the early stages of creating a crystal collection. Its warm orange color is attractive and it feels silky smooth when it is polished. It can be found as carved "worry stones" that can be carried and touched to ease stress and tension. Simple tumblestones in a wonderful variety of shades of orange make a lovely display.

RAW

CARNELIAN

FORM AND STRUCTURE
trigonal with fibrous layers of quartz, creating soft smooth bands of color and a hint of translucence

COLOR
orange in different shades, from pale to deep orange-red; stones can be clear or show a wide variety of specks, stripes, or markings

GEOGRAPHICAL SOURCES
Brazil, India, Iran, Saudi Arabia, Uruguay

RARITY
very easily obtained

HARDNESS
7

PHYSICAL/EMOTIONAL USES
speeds up healing processes, especially after trauma or injury

helps improve elimination and increases vitality and strength

purifies the blood and improves circulation

helps bring courage when facing personal challenges

HEALING EFFECTS
used with rose quartz over the heart, carnelian balances sexual energy with the vibration of love

in healing layouts, placed on the lower abdomen, it energizes the sacral and root chakras

PERSONAL USES
lay on the lower abdomen or lower back, place in the bath, or wear over the heart for warmth and support

THE YELLOW AND GOLD RAY

Bright as sunlight, energizing and expansive, the color yellow symbolizes the full strength of the midday sun at its height. It is a positive ray, stimulating mental clarity and keen observation. It helps with decision making when you need to "see the whole picture." Fresh tones of yellow are instantly brightening and cheering in the home, popular for interior decoration.

Yellow has a cleansing and detoxifying feel about it, clearing away debris to leave a clear space. Yellow fruit, such as lemons and grapefruit, have the same kind of appeal—bright, fresh, reenergizing. They are excellent in the diet to tone the digestive system and help the liver to function well; they also support the immune system, which benefits from the yellow ray in color healing.

This is the color associated with the solar plexus chakra center, situated in the middle of the upper abdomen where the ribs curve upward above the stomach. This chakra is linked to mental activity, expansion, and intellectual analysis, and it improves concentration. However, too much activity in this area can be limiting; the mind does not hold the whole picture when it comes to living one's life. The solar plexus chakra is frequently a site of tension, requiring balance from the heart chakra above, which brings love to the situation, and the sacral chakra below, which helps in relating to others.

26

Golden rays

Gold is a supercharged version of the color yellow. The metal gold is one of the most precious minerals available; it is also a symbol of the sun, not just the physical star in the sky but also the spiritual center of the cosmos. Gold is a beautiful healing ray, universal in its power to transmute negativity. If you are in need of emotional or spiritual comfort, imagine yourself in a shower of golden rays. Feel this transmuting energy. If you believe in angels, then the beauty of gold may speak to you of their presence, as it is traditionally the color of their haloes.

The metal gold and the yellow-colored crystals are a lovely group of minerals, highly attractive to wear and positive in their healing effects. They promote a state of well-being and joy. They reflect light and give a sense of clarity and ease. They promote self-confidence and self-expression in the highest sense. Collect and keep them in the home to increase cleansing and healing energies in your personal space.

YELLOW TIGER'S EYE

Tiger's eye is a name given to a group of stones with a special luminous quality in their structure. They are basically silicon dioxide—quartz— but they have formed in an unusual way, when fibers of a mineral called crocidolite are laid down in parallel bands within the quartz structure. This creates a silky-looking shimmer effect when the stone is turned to the light, resembling a cat's eye. It is sometimes called chatoyancy, after the French word for cat. These stones are hard and can be carved; a wonderful way to appreciate the light effects in tiger's eye is to see a large piece in a polished sphere. Yellow tiger's eye is the most common form of the stone, with bands of gold to yellow-brown reflecting a lovely golden shimmering light.

Tiger's eye has been a popular semiprecious stone for thousands of years. Tombs in the ancient city of Ur in Mesopotamia (modern Iraq) dating back to 2500 BCE have yielded gold set with agates, such as tiger's eye and carnelian. At the time of Alexander the Great in the fourth century BCE, Greek goldsmiths used tiger's eye as one of an extensive range of precious and semiprecious stones set in gold jewelry, including necklaces, rings, and torques.

In healing, tiger's eye is used to shield the energy field, or aura, from negativity, as well as clearing tension and mental blocks from the solar plexus chakra in the center of the upper abdomen. It brings a soothing golden resonance to calm and restore body and mind.

RAW

YELLOW TIGER'S EYE

FORM AND STRUCTURE
trigonal, forming in a hexagonal
pattern

opaque with shimmering layers
of quartz and crocidolite fibers

COLOR
golden yellow, also blue, blue-
green, red (heat treated)

GEOGRAPHICAL SOURCES
India, Myanmar, South Africa,
USA

RARITY
very easily obtained

HARDNESS
7

PHYSICAL/EMOTIONAL USES
linked to the energy of the solar
plexus chakra, clearing mental
blocks and encouraging focus
on current issues

supports a healthy metabolism
and prevents physical energy
from becoming depleted

reputed to keep the eyes healthy
and increase clear vision

HEALING EFFECTS
in healing layouts, place over the
solar plexus area or abdomen to
ease tension and protect from
external influences

use to "anchor" the lower part
of the body as a platform for
spiritual expansion

PERSONAL USES
hold a tumblestone in each hand
and meditate on the golden
quality of tiger's eye

THE GREEN RAY

This is the richest, most lush shade of green, seen at its most beautiful in the vegetation of the tropics. The reason why plants are at their most green in tropical locations is because they have maximum access to the sun at its height, being closer to the equator. Provided they have enough water, the power of intense sunlight acting on plant tissues produces the most incredible emerald shades of green; this is the process of photosynthesis—the miracle of light creating food for plants—at its best.

This vibrant green is a symbol of growth, expansion, power, and vitality. It is no coincidence that the Aztec and Inca peoples of Central and South America valued green stones such as emerald and jade—these were visible symbols taken out of the earth that echoed the lush vegetation of their own surroundings. Green is also a powerful color to the Maori people of New Zealand, whose lands are filled with abundant plant life. Green as a color is used directly on the body in healing to help speed up regrowth of damaged tissues, and even to help heal broken bones. It helps to infuse body and mind with transformative energy, creating possibilities to move forward.

A bridge between body and soul

In the chakra system, green is the principal color associated with the heart. In the system of seven major chakras, the heart center is in the middle. Below it are the warmer vibrations of yellow (solar plexus), orange (sacrum), and red (base of spine); above the heart are the cooler vibrations of blue (throat), indigo (third eye), and violet (crown). Green is the bridge between these different energy levels; the energy of the heart chakra bridges the demands of the physical body, symbolized by the lower chakras, and the aspirations of the spirit, centered in the upper chakras. It does that by enabling the expression of love, which in its purest form balances all things.

Green is a good color to bring into your life when you feel a need for something new, when you want to break out of an old routine that no longer serves you, or when you are ready to start a new relationship. In medieval times, there was a French saying, *Il te faudra de vert vestir, c'est la livrée aux amoureux*, which means "You must dress in green, it is the livery [an old word for costume or uniform] of lovers."

AVENTURINE

Green aventurine is a form of microcrystalline quartz containing particles of mica, a mineral that creates a sparkling sheen, so the stone glistens as it is turned to the light. All over the world its hardness has made it a popular choice for carving; in India—one of the main sources of green aventurine—it is made into beads, jewelry, boxes, and intricate figurines. Because it forms in massive blocks, this stone is also popular in interior and exterior mosaics, as flooring or internal cladding in combination with marble. In Russia, it was used after the 1880s by the Russian jeweler Fabergé, along with other semiprecious and precious stones—including jasper, lapis lazuli, quartz, jade, and sapphire—to make the famous Fabergé eggs.

Aventurine is an inexpensive and popular choice for starting a collection of crystals. Small polished stones have a smooth and silky feel. Darker specimens tend to have more mica particles, and lighter stones are more opaque. The name aventurine is from the Italian *a ventura*, which means "by chance"; this name is also given to goldstone, a form of sparkling Italian glass invented in the eighteenth century.

In crystal healing, green aventurine is used to clear away negative emotional patterns and support the heart chakra; it also calms powerful feelings in the lower abdomen, such as anger, centered on the solar plexus chakra. Aventurine encourages the expression of gratitude, hope, and positive approaches to life. It can also help to neutralize geopathic or electromagnetic stress.

POLISHED

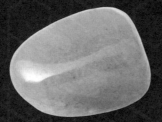

AVENTURINE

FORM AND STRUCTURE
trigonal system, microcrystalline quartz in massive formations

easily carved, and when polished has a silky feel

COLOR
mostly green with specks of sparkling fuchsite, also red, blue

GEOGRAPHICAL SOURCES
Brazil, India, Russia

RARITY
easily obtained

HARDNESS
7

PHYSICAL/EMOTIONAL USES
supports the system after a period of illness—encourages tissue repair and healing

supports the heart and circulation

encourages optimism and a renewed zest for life, as well as gratitude for what has been received

an excellent stone to destress and calm body and mind

HEALING EFFECTS
in healing layouts, can be placed over the heart chakra or the lower abdomen to clear negativity and encourage harmony

its energy is gentle and supportive

PERSONAL USES
carry with you as a stone of harmony

meditate with aventurine to take stock of where you are and where you would like to be

THE SAPPHIRE BLUE RAY

This is the deep sapphire blue seen in many medieval paintings and stained-glass windows, the translucent shade most famously featured in the cathedral of Chartres in France. The interior of this vast stone building is kept deliberately dim, so that when light passes through the windows, the depth and beauty of the blue glass is particularly noticeable. Medieval glassworkers used ground lapis lazuli to stain glass that particular color, and artists used the same powder in mixing paint to show the Virgin Mary's robes.

The world-famous illuminated manuscript, *Les Très Riches Heures du Duc de Berry*, produced in France in the early fifteenth century, is full of wonderful paintings showing this lapis-lazuli blue in the skies, the backgrounds, and the rich clothing of the nobility. From medieval times through to the Renaissance, this shade of blue was a symbol of heaven. This ray is also traditionally associated with Archangel Michael, whose mantle is often depicted in that color. Michael is a warrior-archangel with a flaming sword, a symbol of the sparkling awakening of the soul. Meditating on the deep blue ray is a wonderful way to connect with the angel's energy.

The color of self-expression

Crystals and minerals with this deep blue color have been worn since
antiquity by kings, potentates, and spiritual leaders. Today they can
be worn and possessed by everyone; they help to awaken leadership
qualities within you, showing you the nature of your unique gifts. It is
easy to "hide your light under a bushel," but every person has a unique
quality, and wearing deep blue crystals helps you gain confidence in
communicating whatever your individual gifts may be. Sapphire blue
is the luminous shade of the throat chakra, the place of self-expression.
This means tapping into your creativity, bringing into the world the gifts
you hold, enabling them to serve a higher purpose. Imagine a world
where creativity and individual expression were encouraged and truly
valued in every child and adult. How might that world be? We admire
the geniuses in our history books, but the ability to create lies in each
and every one of us. The sapphire blue ray connects us to our deepest
dreams and helps us make them come alive.

SODALITE

Sodalite is made up of sodium aluminum silicate chloride; it gets its name from its sodium content. It is a rich, royal blue color interspersed with white veins; good-quality pieces when polished look similar to lapis lazuli. However, it does not contain the pyrite inclusions found in the latter. Another way to tell the two apart is that sodalite is more brittle; clear lines in its structure show potential breaking points. It rarely forms crystals, and it is usually found in massive granular formations or fillings in veins in igneous rocks. One source of rare but particularly fine crystalline sodalite is the region around the volcano Vesuvius in southern Italy; massive deposits are also found in Ontario, Canada. Today, sodalite is used with jasper, marble, and other fine masonry stones to create elaborate interiors, staircases, and floors for important buildings, its blue color providing an attractive contrast.

Sodalite is used in crystal healing to expand the mind and encourage clear thinking; it is also a good stone to work with if you are trying to establish a regular meditation practice. It helps to connect your physical self to your spiritual self so that you can move easily between different levels of consciousness. Its deep blue color brings peace and tranquility to your environment and soothes unruly emotions. It also enhances your intuition, that sixth sense that encourages creativity and spontaneity.

POLISHED

RAW

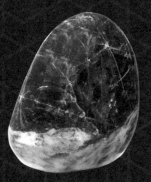

SODALITE

FORM AND STRUCTURE
cubic system in massive or granular formations, rarely crystalline

often occurs in igneous rocks

when polished has a waxy feel

COLOR
mostly royal blue, also white, gray, green

GEOGRAPHICAL SOURCES
Canada, Greenland, Italy, Myanmar, Russia, USA

RARITY
easily obtained as small tumblestones

HARDNESS
6

PHYSICAL/EMOTIONAL USES
calms the mind and helps relaxation

assists the third-eye chakra to focus in meditation

helps support the immune system, clearing problems in the throat and sinuses, and soothes the voice, especially if the vocal chords are strained

helps clear feelings of internal conflict or lack of certainty, encouraging self-confidence in personal expression

HEALING EFFECTS
place over the throat or third eye between the eyebrows, whichever feels appropriate, to clear negative feelings and increase relaxation in the system

place over the heart chakra with a piece of rose quartz to create a fusion of intuition and unconditional love

PERSONAL USES
meditate with it to improve your ability to let go of everyday concerns and focus on just being

THE DARK PURPLE RAY

Dark purple is a rich color that has been esteemed since ancient times as a mark of high rank and even royalty. Archeological evidence from Crete, home of the Minoan culture, has shown that extraction of what came to be known as Tyrian purple was taking place there as far back as 2000 BCE. Tyrian purple was a dye from the mucous membranes of particular mollusks, obtained using a process that even modern methods have been unable to replicate. In Roman times, the city of Tyre in the eastern Mediterranean was a key producing area, hence the name Tyrian.

Apart from yellow saffron, this purple dye was one of the most expensive and rare coloring ingredients of the ancient world. In consequence, it was reserved for the robes, cloaks, and togas of persons of highest rank, and even though it disappeared from use over time, superseded by plant dyes such as woad or mallow, the color purple remained a sign of high status. To this day purple still has a regal quality about it.

This rich purple shade is also associated with the crown chakra, the energy center that sits at the top of the skull. This is often represented in religious paintings as a golden light or halo around the top of the head. Purple is the color that activates it. The meaning of the crown chakra is that each and every one of us has the opportunity to achieve our highest potential on all levels—mental, physical, emotional, and spiritual—during our lifetime.

Experience an awakening

Activation of the crown chakra is a crowning moment in life, signaling
the awakening of divine purpose in an individual. Unlike in the past,
when such potential was reserved only for a few, now there is recognition
that such awakening can be experienced by all. Moments of ecstatic
understanding, flashes of blinding intuition or inspiration, bursts of
enlightened creativity that seem to come from nowhere are all signs of
the crown chakra opening. These moments need to be balanced by being
firmly grounded. A wise Buddhist saying states: "Before enlightenment,
chopping wood and carrying water; after enlightenment, chopping wood
and carrying water." As human beings, we operate on all levels, physical
as well as spiritual. The key thing is balance.

Purple crocus flowers in the spring illustrate this deep color so well;
they contrast with the rich shade of new grass, showing the abundance
of heart-chakra green against the rich purple of crown-chakra wisdom.

AMETHYST

One of the best known and most beautiful of all crystals, amethyst occurs in a great variety of shades, shapes, and sizes. It is a form of quartz, colored by different amounts of iron or aluminum. It occurs in deep dark purple shades right through to pale lilac, depending on where it is found. It can be found in large defined crystal points or in clusters of smaller terminations. Another typical and large form of amethyst occurs inside pockets (vugs) within volcanic rock, where an enclosed space has been created as the rock cooled. These formations have a greenish encrustation on the outside, and when split open reveal hundreds of amethyst crystals growing toward the center of the space. Entire pieces are available—and expensive—to buy; they look like crystal caves, and can be as much as 3 feet (1 meter) in size.

The word *amethyst* is derived from an Ancient Greek term meaning "not drunk"; the Modern Greek word *amethystos* still means both amethyst and sober. Quite why the stone was given this name is unclear, although its deep purple color resembles wine. Amethyst has been prized since ancient times, used in royal jewelry such as crowns and scepters, and in the Old Testament book of *Exodus* it is mentioned as one of the stones in the breastplate of Aaron the High Priest.

POLISHED

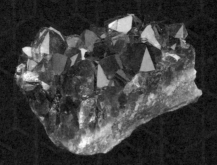

AMETHYST

FORM AND STRUCTURE
trigonal crystal system, forming long prismatic crystals with a six-sided pyramid at the point; also smaller clusters or large, enclosed masses (vugs) within metamorphic rocks

COLOR
dark vivid purple, in a variety of shades, to pale lilac

GEOGRAPHICAL SOURCES
Africa, Brazil, Canada, Mexico, Russia, USA

RARITY
easily obtained in a variety of shapes and sizes

HARDNESS
7

PHYSICAL/EMOTIONAL USES
popular as a purifying crystal, helping to ward off negative influences and protect from environmental stress

calms the nervous system and the brain, easing headaches and migraines

opens the third-eye and crown chakras, enhancing personal spiritual awareness

HEALING EFFECTS
in crystal-healing layouts, place over the top of the head or on the third eye to expand conscious awareness

place a circle of eight pieces of amethyst around the body to create a protective field

PERSONAL USES
wear or carry amethyst to help calm mental stress

place under the pillow to improve the quality of sleep

Crystals Gallery

The following pages show a wonderful collection of images of many kinds of crystals in all their colors and beauty. These pages are a visual treasure chest to be enjoyed and explored.

Looking at these images may inspire you in different ways. For example, you may be drawn to crystals of a certain color and feel that you would like to have a particular stone with you as a result. On the other hand, you may be looking for a particular type of crystal and this gallery will show you examples so that you can recognize specimens in stores. You may also be given a crystal and wish to check what kind it is—again, the gallery is a good place to start looking so you can identify the stone.

The world of crystals is fascinating, diverse and magical. Their physical qualities—some geometric, some metallic, some transparent, some opaque, some filled with reflections and some dark and mysterious—are all displayed here for you to see.

BROWN

SMOKY QUARTZ

PETRIFIED WOOD

BROWN JASPER

RED

GARNET

RUBY

RED TIGER'S EYE

RED JASPER

ZINCITE

SPINEL

ORANGE

ORANGE CALCITE

ARAGONITE

CARNELIAN

YELLOW AND GOLD

SUNSTONE

COPPER

GOLDEN TOPAZ

CITRINE

AMBER

YELLOW TIGER'S EYE

YELLOW JASPER

SULFUR

CHRYSOBERYL

PYRITE

GOLD

GOLDEN GREEN

PERIDOT

CHROME DIOPSIDE

SERPENTINE

PALE GREEN

APOPHYLITE

45

PREHNITE

GREEN CALCITE

GREEN

EMERALD

AVENTURINE

GREEN FLUORITE

JADE

MALACHITE

DARK GREEN

MOLDAVITE

MOSS AGATE

CRYSTALS GALLERY

46

BLUE-GREEN

SERAPHINITE

TURQUOISE

LABRADORITE

APATITE

AMAZONITE

CHRYSOCOLLA

PALE BLUE-GREEN

PALE BLUE

AQUAMARINE

CHRYSOPRASE

BLUE LACE AGATE

BLUE MOONSTONE

CHALCEDONY

KYANITE

SAPPHIRE BLUE

CELESTITE

LAPIS LAZULI

SODALITE

DARK BLUE

BLUE SAPPHIRE

AZURITE

IOLITE

CRYSTALS GALLERY

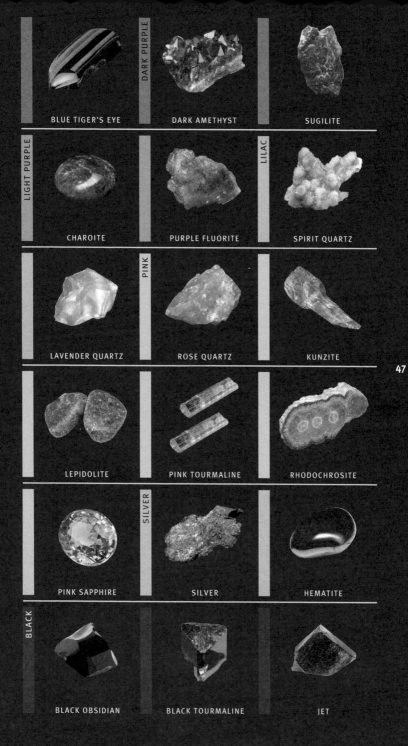

DARK PURPLE

BLUE TIGER'S EYE

DARK AMETHYST

SUGILITE

LIGHT PURPLE

LILAC

CHAROITE

PURPLE FLUORITE

SPIRIT QUARTZ

PINK

LAVENDER QUARTZ

ROSE QUARTZ

KUNZITE

47

LEPIDOLITE

PINK TOURMALINE

RHODOCHROSITE

SILVER

PINK SAPPHIRE

SILVER

HEMATITE

BLACK

BLACK OBSIDIAN

BLACK TOURMALINE

JET

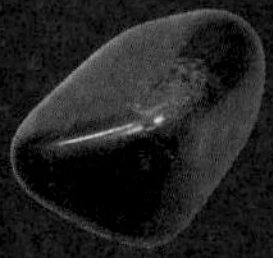

ONYX

WHITE MOONSTONE

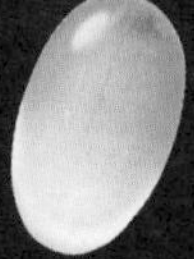

SELENITE

DIAMOND

DANBURITE

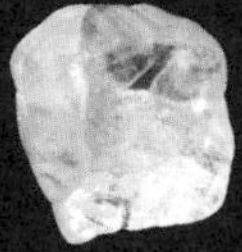

AZEZTULITE

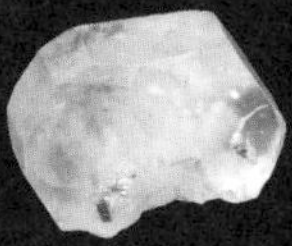

48

PHENACITE

CLEAR QUARTZ

DOUBLE-TERMINATED

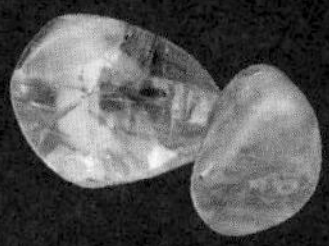

RUTILATED
CLEAR QUARTZ

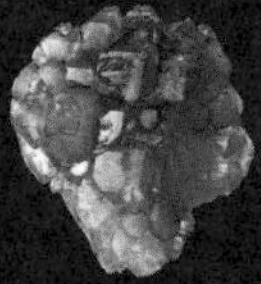

ELESTIAL

PHANTOM

LASER WAND

MANIFESTATION

SELF-HEALED

GENERATOR

SOUL-MATE

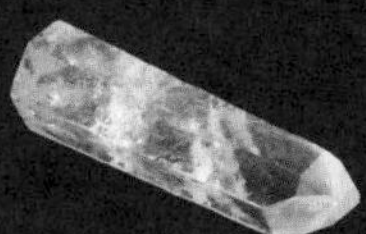

CHANNELING

CATHEDRAL

RECORD-KEEPER

ABUNDANCE

COMBINATIONS

LEMURIAN-SEED

RHODONITE

PIETERSITE

WATERMELON
TOURMALINE

GREEN-AND-PURPLE
FLUORITE

TOURMALINATED
QUARTZ

49

AMETRINE

PEARL

BLOODSTONE

SNOWFLAKE OBSIDIAN

RAINBOW OBSIDIAN

OPAL

MERLINITE

OCEAN JASPER

Crystals in Your Life

Crystals add wonderful qualities to life: their beauty enhances personal space, their colors attract the eye, their energy communicates a sense of presence. In this chapter, ways to choose and care for crystals will be shown, as well as many different approaches to their practical use. Building a collection of crystals is a very satisfying hobby; understanding their significance as well as their physical attributes adds new levels of fascination to the subject.

By placing crystals in your home or work environment, by carrying them or wearing them as jewelry, or by meditating with them, we can find many more ways of experiencing their helpful effects.

Simple approaches to crystal healing will also be shown as a starting point. These are intended for use with a friend as a way of exploring how crystals affect energy. This requires sensitivity and openness, as well as trust and helpful communication between both parties, so that the experience of using the crystals is positive and beneficial. Expressing what feels good and what does not is an important part of the exchange. Working with crystals encourages the development of new levels of intuition and creativity

Choosing, cleansing, and caring for crystals

Crystals can be bought in many different locations, including New Age stores, specialist crystal suppliers, and crystal exhibitions or fairs. The more specialized the outlet, the bigger the choice of crystals available and the likelihood that stock will be of good quality. Serious crystal collectors will look for a reputable supplier who knows the geographical origin of the stones as well as correctly identifying them.

Different types of crystal are typically available:

CRYSTAL CLUSTERS • these are made up of many small crystals emerging from a common base; a good example is amethyst

SINGLE CRYSTAL POINTS • these tend to be pieces of quartz, and a good supplier will name them individually if they have specialist labels such as phantom, cathedral, generator, etc. (*see pages 230–37*)

LARGE UNPOLISHED PIECES • common examples are rose quartz or aventurine, and these work well placed outside

TUMBLESTONES • these are small shiny crystal pebbles polished with gravel; they are the cheapest form of crystal and are popular with children

SHAPED CRYSTALS • these can be pieces of quartz that have been carved into particular shapes, such as the rose quartz or citrine flame shaped pieces that are becoming popular, or carved polished spheres in different sizes

MINERALOGICAL SPECIMENS • these are often delicate—sulfur or copper, for example—and may be presented in boxes

For healing purposes, small clusters, single points, or tumblestones are the best choice.

SINGLE CRYSTAL POINT

UNPOLISHED

TUMBLESTONES

CLEANSING CRYSTALS

When you buy a crystal it is a good idea to wash any dust off it with lukewarm soapy water and then pat it dry. This simply cleans away surface dust, but there is another level on which crystals need to be cleansed using energy, which prepares them for use in healing and also programs them to your individual frequency. There are two steps to this. First, use one of the following methods to clear the crystal matrix:

• place the crystal under cold running water for a few moments
• strike a tuning fork or small bell beside it to cleanse it with sound
• light some incense and pass it through the smoke.

Second, hold the crystal in your left hand and place your right hand over the top of it. Then close your eyes, breathe deeply, and focus your energy. Say: "May the energy of Divine Love infuse this crystal so it works for the highest good."

This process clears and prepares the crystal to amplify and enhance energy beneficially in your life.

53

CARING FOR CRYSTALS

Crystals need to be looked after, so when you buy a stone, check its profile. Here are some simple tips to bear in mind:

• if it is soft, like amber, it needs to be kept away from harder crystals that could scratch it
• avoid knocking quartz crystal points or they will shatter
• many crystals, such as amethyst, will fade in color if exposed to strong sunlight, so they are best kept in the shade
• small crystals—Herkimer diamond or spinel, for example—are best kept safe in a box
• precious stones, such as opal, and organic minerals, such as pearl, need to be kept wrapped in a soft cloth and away from heat to prevent scratching or shattering.

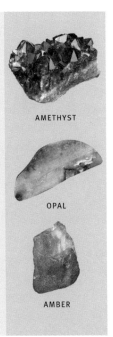

AMETHYST

OPAL

AMBER

Crystal meditation

Meditation is an art that balances the entire chakra system, opening the way to inner peace and harmony. There are many different forms of meditation, all of them offering the potential to reach a state of spiritual enlightenment. Meditation in its purest sense is not allied to any particular religion; it is simply a practice that enables spiritual development. It is found in the teachings of many ancient traditions, including Zen Buddhism and Hinduism.

Meditation is not a quick fix, it is an art that takes time to learn and absorb. Practiced over a period of time it brings real benefits, such as lowered blood pressure, a calmer mind, and less turbulent emotions. Regular practice is the key to success. Twenty minutes a day is a good starting point, and the best time to do it is first thing in the morning. Either sit on a hard-backed chair with your legs uncrossed and feet on the floor, hands loosely clasped in your lap, or sit cross-legged on the floor in a meditation posture.

FOCUSING ON A CRYSTAL

Using a crystal is another aspect of meditation practice where the energy of the crystal itself can contribute to the experience. Selecting a crystal for meditation is entirely your own choice. You may be drawn to a stone because of its color, shape, or feel. You may have read about a stone and decided you want to work with it. You may simply look at your collection and feel that one particular piece jumps out at you.

There are two simple ways to meditate with a stone. The first is to gaze at it. Meditation with eyes focusing on an object is a technique from Zen tradition, where contemplation stills the mind. If you decide to try this method, set the stone on a plain cloth on a clean surface, with a lit candle beside it. Settle yourself in the meditation pose and breathe rhythmically as you relax. Let your eyes rest on the stone and focus on it for as long as you can without looking away. If you need to do so, look at the candle for a moment, then back at the stone. Notice any thoughts, feelings, or impressions that come to you and then let them flow away. After your twenty minutes, write notes to recall any important details.

MAINTAINING BALANCE

The second way is to hold the crystal in your left hand and cover it with your right. The left hand is receptive and the right hand dynamic, and by holding the crystal between them in this way the yin-yang balance of energy is maintained. Relax, close your eyes, and breathe calmly. Simply let

ABOVE *Holding crystals is a way to relate to them individually; you may feel warmth or tingling in your body, in chakra areas such as the third eye or the crown.*

your mind rest and focus on the stone between your hands. Notice how it feels, how you feel. You may notice sensations of warmth or tingling in your hands or elsewhere in the body. This is the energy of the crystal interacting with your own. After breathing deeply and coming out of the meditation, make notes of any important impressions.

Crystals in the environment

Crystals can play a big part in maintaining positive clear energy in the environment. They can be placed indoors or outdoors in order to enjoy their effects. Deciding where to put a crystal is an individual choice, and intuition will guide you to the most appropriate location. Some crystal healers say stones like to be moved around; every so often you may sense a need to vary their position—and if so, just do it!

INSIDE

Inside buildings, crystals bring sparkling light to a space, as well as different colors and also the special properties they hold. Here are some ideas to try in different rooms:

In the office/workspace • Computers, telephones, or mobile phones that receive and emit electromagnetic and radio waves are sources of environmental stress. Placing neutralizing and cleansing crystals such as smoky quartz, black tourmaline, jet or obsidian in the office, on top of computers or phones, will absorb negative waves or radiation and channel them back into the earth.

JET

RAINBOW FLUORITE

In a bedroom • Keeping crystals in the bedroom is a matter of personal choice. Some, including zincite, have a lively energy and might interfere with sleep patterns. Even clear quartz crystals can be too intense for some. Softer versions of quartz, such as amethyst, rose quartz, or aventurine, have a gentler effect and can improve your sleep if placed under the pillow.

ORANGE CALCITE

BLUE CHALCEDONY

In a meditation space • If you have a space dedicated to meditation, yoga, or healing, then placing crystals is a wonderful way to enhance the energy there— again, use your intuition to guide your choice. For example, clusters of quartz or amethyst, pieces of orange or green calcite, blue chalcedony, or colorful green-and-purple fluorite will all share their healing energies in the space, preparing for relaxation and spiritual development.

OUTSIDE

Outside in the open air, crystals can also add special energy. Here are some ideas for placing crystals in outside spaces:

In the garden • Crystals can be placed among plants to enhance their energies—green stones, such as aventurine or moss agate, are particularly good to use because of their color and their reputed ability to enhance the energy matrix of nature. Large pieces can be obtained, and these are particularly suited to outdoor spaces where they become special features in the garden landscape.

In water • Water features are becoming more popular in gardens, and adding combinations of crystals to a fountain or flowing display adds even more color and sparkle. Rose quartz, green or orange calcite, or a display of multicolored pieces of jasper is lovely to try.

In a sacred space • Special garden spaces are also becoming popular, such as circular paved areas, maybe with a fire pit, or a planted area around a hot tub, or a special outdoor meditation space. Small crystal tumblestones lend themselves to the creation of outdoor mosaics in order to completely individualize a space.

ABOVE *Sparkling with light, crystals bring an enhanced sense of beauty to an outdoor space, and create an atmosphere of peace and harmony.*

Wearing crystals for healing

Wearing jewelry is something many of us take completely for granted; something we do to accessorize our clothes, something that makes us feel good. However, do we ever stop to consider what we choose to wear as jewelry and why? Might there be a deeper significance behind the kinds of jewelry we choose? In the Bible, in the book of *Exodus*, God gives instructions for the manufacture of a breastplate for his high priest, Aaron. It contains precious stones such as topaz, agate, emerald, diamond, sapphire, amethyst, and beryl. This account shows that these precious stones together denote the rank and status of the high priest, and also point to his spiritual power. Religious leaders, kings, queens, princes, and potentates of the ancient world wore special jewelry not just for show, but to demonstrate their role as intermediaries with the spiritual realms. Such cultures as the Ancient Egyptians even decked out their high-ranking dead in these items of ritual jewelry so they would be recognized in the next life.

This may seem a long way from modern life, but we do have access to an extremely wide selection of precious and semiprecious stones these days, and they are available to everyone. Study and appreciation of their qualities can lead to a greater awareness of why they are being worn.

JEWELRY CRYSTALS

Here is a list of some typical crystals that may be chosen as jewelry for energetic reasons:

ROSE QUARTZ • to enhance unconditional love

CITRINE • to energize the mind

IOLITE • to inspire creativity

AMETHYST • to relax the mind

LAPIS LAZULI • to expand the third eye

AMBER • to enhance reproductive energy

MOLDAVITE • to encourage transformation

CLEAR QUARTZ • to keep a clear focus

MOONSTONE • to balance the hormones

CLEAR QUARTZ

Wearing crystals is a convenient and simple way to enjoy their effects. Set in gold or silver, precious and pure metal elements that contain the crystalline energies perfectly, these crystals are no longer simply ornamentation. They are healing tools that enhance and revitalize the energy field of the wearer. This is why sometimes it does not feel right to wear crystal jewelry that has belonged to someone else; that person's energy frequency will still be around it. If the piece is cleaned properly and reprogramed (*see pages 52–53*) then it will feel different and can be worn by another person.

ABOVE *Wearing crystals brings their energy directly into contact with the skin; they bring pleasure because they are beautiful objects and have healing effects.*

The most effective type of jewelry to choose for healing purposes is a pendant that hangs down toward the heart. The heart is a bridging chakra between spirit and matter, and combinations of crystals work well there to spread their energy throughout the auric field. Crystals can also be placed in a small pouch attached to a cord and worn around the neck, hanging over the chest to keep special stones close to the heart.

Crystals for physical health

Many crystals are considered to help particular physical conditions. The associations are sometimes linked to ancient healing traditions, or to more modern uses of crystals in healing practice. It is important to stress that keeping, holding, or using a crystal associated with a condition is no replacement for conventional medical advice. Any persistent conditions or changes in physical symptoms should be reported to your doctor. However, having an appropriate crystal with you allows its energy to support you in your healing process.

HEALING CRYSTALS

ALLERGIC REACTIONS • hematite, bloodstone, rose quartz

ANEMIA • garnet, bloodstone, hematite

ASTHMA • malachite, rhodochrosite, chrysocolla

BACKACHE • amber, citrine, danburite

BACTERIAL INFECTIONS • sulfur, malachite, aventurine

BLADDER PROBLEMS • prehnite, amber, orange calcite

BLOOD CIRCULATION • red jasper, bloodstone, hematite

BLOOD PURIFICATION • ruby, garnet, malachite, aventurine

BOWEL PROBLEMS • lepidolite, peridot, green fluorite

BROKEN BONES • calcite (any color), azurite, fluorite (any color)

CANCER SUPPORT • rose quartz, sugilite, watermelon tourmaline

CHRONIC FATIGUE SYNDROME • ruby, amber, aventurine, amethyst

CONSTIPATION • smoky/rutilated smoky quartz, black tourmaline

DETOXIFICATION • smoky quartz, sulfur, malachite

DIGESTIVE PROBLEMS • green fluorite, amber, citrine

EATING DISORDERS • rose quartz, kunzite, watermelon tourmaline

ENVIRONMENTAL POLLUTION • smoky quartz, zincite, merlinite

EYE PROBLEMS • aquamarine, blue chalcedony, blue tiger's eye

FERTILITY (to improve) • rose quartz, garnet, blue moonstone

FIBROMYALGIA • amethyst, aventurine, blue lace agate

FOOT PROBLEMS • black onyx, smoky quartz, prehnite

HEADACHES • rose quartz, blue lace agate, aquamarine

HEART ORGAN ISSUES • lavender quartz, rhodochrosite, garnet

The list below is by no means exhaustive; it suggests possible crystals in each context. The ways to use these stones are those already featured in this book, such as holding, carrying, or wearing a crystal, or using a crystal in the bath. Any crystal can also be placed over the relevant part of the body and left there for about fifteen minutes to feel its effect. If meditating with a particular crystal, ask to be shown any relevant information to the condition you are experiencing. Repeat any treatment as needed.

HIGH BLOOD PRESSURE • amethyst, chrysocolla, blue chalcedony

HORMONE BALANCE • amber, blue moonstone, carnelian

IMMUNE SUPPORT • Herkimer diamond, aventurine, rutilated clear quartz

JOINT SORENESS • green calcite, azurite, rhodonite

KIDNEY SUPPORT • aquamarine, orange calcite, smoky quartz

LIVER SUPPORT • carnelian, red jasper, charoite

LUNG SUPPORT • lapis lazuli, turquoise, rhodonite

MENOPAUSE SUPPORT • blue moonstone, carnelian, amber

MENSTRUAL SUPPORT • bloodstone, white moonstone, carnelian

MUSCLE ACHES • hematite, danburite, red jasper

OSTEOPOROSIS • calcite (any color), fluorite (any color), azurite

PREMENSTRUAL SYNDROME • amber, blue moonstone, kunzite

REPRODUCTIVE ORGANS (f) • chrysoprase, blue moonstone, golden topaz

REPRODUCTIVE ORGANS (m) • jade, chrysoprase, carnelian

SCIATICA • jade, lapis lazuli, amethyst

SKELETAL SUPPORT • amazonite, fluorite, pyrite

SKIN ISSUES • rose quartz, azurite, citrine

SORE THROAT • angelite, celestite, blue lace agate

SURGICAL RECOVERY • amber, rose quartz, chrysoprase

TEETH PROBLEMS • calcite (any color), selenite, fluorite (any color)

THYROID SUPPORT • citrine, aquamarine, lapis lazuli

VARICOSE VEIN SUPPORT • amber, bloodstone, snowflake obsidian

WATER RETENTION • hematite, citrine, smoky quartz

Crystals for psychological health

This list of crystal correspondences links to moods, feelings, and mental attitude. The use of crystals to soothe the mind is another ancient practice; thousands of years ago, in India, particular crystals were linked to deities and accredited with different mental powers. Modern crystal healing suggests that psychological associations with crystals are individual; crystals are attractive because of their color, light reflections, or shape, and tend to represent levels of energy that are missing in a person's life, which they can then replenish.

CRYSTALS AND THE MIND

ADDICTION RECOVERY • malachite, peridot, smoky quartz

ANGER • rhodonite, chrysocolla, lapis lazuli

ANXIETY • rose quartz, amethyst, aventurine

ASSERTIVENESS (to encourage) • citrine, yellow tiger's eye, sodalite

ATTENTION DEFICIT DISORDER • kunzite, selenite, azurite

BREATHLESSNESS (stress) • amber, seraphinite, green calcite

BURN OUT • ruby, garnet, carnelian

COMMUNICATION ISSUES • turquoise, lapis lazuli, angelite

CONFIDENCE (lack of) • citrine, amber, orange calcite

CONFUSION • fluorite (any color), charoite, lepidolite

COURAGE (to build) • bloodstone, hematite, yellow tiger's eye

CREATIVITY (to encourage) • iolite, phenakite, cathedral quartz

DEPRESSION (to ease) • amethyst, angelite, kunzite, pink tourmaline

DREAMS (to calm) • rose quartz, blue lace agate, prehnite

DREAMS (to encourage recall) • Herkimer diamond, labradorite, elestial quartz

DRUG ABUSE RECOVERY • smoky quartz, jet, rutilated clear quartz

EATING DISORDERS • rose quartz, kunzite, watermelon tourmaline

EMOTIONAL DISTRESS • lavender quartz, carnelian, purple fluorite

FATIGUE • amethyst, aventurine, seraphinite

FEAR • angelite, kyanite, lepidolite

FOCUS (to build) • fluorite (any color), calcite (any color), selenite

FORGIVENESS • kunzite, rose quartz, chrysoprase

If you are experiencing a feeling or a mood and a particular crystal jumps out at you, then understand that this is the one that is suited to your current needs. Follow your impulse and allow that crystal's energy to interact with yours. It should also be said that crystals are not necessarily a miracle cure, and if you are experiencing repeated emotional patterns and feelings of unhappiness then it is important to seek professional guidance. Crystal energies will support you in your healing journey, whether you carry them or wear them.

GRIEF • rainbow obsidian, sugilite, rutilated smoky quartz

GROUNDING • jet, smoky quartz, black tourmaline

GUILT (to ease) • amazonite, aventurine, rose quartz

HYSTERIA • obsidian, hematite, smoky quartz

IMPOTENCE/LACK OF SEXUAL INTEREST • zincite, ruby, carnelian

INFERTILITY (emotional support) • pink tourmaline, ametrine, purple fluorite

INSOMNIA • amethyst, lavender quartz, iolite

IRRITABILITY (to calm) • angelite, blue chalcedony, lepidolite

JEALOUSY (to ease) • peridot, prehnite, citrine

JOY (to increase) • kunzite, sunstone, goldstone

LONELINESS (to ease) • carnelian, amber, orange calcite

LOVE (to bring into life) • ruby, rose quartz, emerald

MEDITATION (to improve focus) • lapis lazuli, iolite, Azeztulite

MEMORY PROBLEMS • green fluorite, amethyst, selenite

NERVOUS TENSION (to ease) • sodalite, watermelon tourmaline, carnelian

PEACE (to encourage) • angelite, seraphinite, pink sapphire

PROTECTION • bloodstone, spinel, hematite

PSYCHIC DEVELOPMENT • lapis lazuli, iolite, channeling quartz

RELATIONSHIPS (to improve) • kyanite, kunzite, peridot

RELAXATION (to increase) • rose quartz, green calcite, blue lace agate

SELF-ESTEEM (to improve) • citrine, amber, ruby

SHYNESS (to decrease) • sunstone, orange calcite, zincite

TRAUMA RECOVERY • aventurine, citrine, chrysocolla

ABOUT THE AUTHOR

JENNIE HARDING BA TIDHA MIPTI HNC has twenty years' experience as a healer working with various modalities including crystals, essential oils, herbs, crystal energy remedies, incense, and natural approaches to beauty. She is the author of fifteen books on this range of topics. Between 1992 and 2005 she was senior Essential Oil Therapeutics tutor at the Tisserand Aromatherapy Institute. She practises Jin Shin Jyutsu, a Japanese energy-balancing art and teaches it as self-help. She dedicates her energy to creating and sharing tools for personal transformation and self-awareness, with a firm belief in self-empowerment and preparation for planetary change.